1.

- - 1

Summary..3

Chapter 2..6

Chapter 1: Understanding OCD in Young Boys..........9

Chapter 2: The Impact of OCD on Daily Life............18

Chapter 3: Building a Supportive Home Environment
....28

Chapter 4: Professional Help and Collaboration........37

Chapter 5: Empowering Young Boys with OCD.......47

Chapter 6: Treatment Approaches for OCD...............56

Chapter 7: Addressing Misconceptions and Stigma...66

Chapter 8: Community Resources and Support.........75

Chapter 9: Navigating School Life............................84

Chapter 10: Lifestyle Management 93

Chapter 11: Long-Term Management of OCD........101

Chapter 12: Stories of Hope and Recovery..............111

Synopsis..119

2.

3.

4.

5.

6.

7.

8.

9.

10.

11.

12.

13.

14.

15.

16.

Summary

Chapter 1: Understanding OCD in Young Boys
3

1.1 Introduction to Obsessive Compulsive Disorder
3

1.2 Symptoms and Diagnosis in Boys
5

1.3 Causes and Manifestations
7

Chapter 2: The Impact of OCD on Daily Life
9

2.1 Emotional Well-being and Social Interactions
9

2.2 Challenges in Thoughts and Behaviors
11

2.3 The Role of Family and School
13

Chapter 3: Building a Supportive Home Environment
15

3.1 Fostering Resilience and Positive Coping Mechanisms
15

3.2 Communication Strategies for Parents and Caregivers

17

3.3 Creating Routine and Structure

19

Chapter 4: Professional Help and Collaboration

21

4.1 Seeking Expert Assistance

21

4.2 Advocating for Educational Accommodations

23

4.3 Working with Therapists and Medical Professionals

25

Chapter 5: Empowering Young Boys with OCD

27

5.1 Understanding the Condition

27

5.2 Communicating Experiences

29

5.3 Participating in Treatment Plans

31

Chapter 6: Treatment Approaches for OCD

33

6.1 Cognitive-Behavioral Therapy (CBT) 33

6.2 Exposure-Response Prevention (ERP) 35

6.3 Mindfulness and Relaxation Exercises 37

Chapter 7: Addressing Misconceptions and Stigma

39

7.1 Debunking Common Myths about OCD

39

7.2 Challenging Societal Stigmas

41

7.3 Promoting Open Dialogue about Mental Health

42

Chapter 8: Community Resources and Support

44

8.1 Finding Support Groups

44

8.2 Utilizing Online Forums

46

8.3 Educational Workshops for Families

48

Chapter 9: Navigating School Life

50

9.1 Collaborating with Educators

50

9.2 Implementing Individualized Education Plans (IEPs)

52

9.3 Social Integration Strategies

Chapter 10: Lifestyle Management ... 54

10.1 Diet, Exercise, and Sleep Hygiene ... 56

10.2 Managing Screen Time ... 56

10.3 Encouraging Hobbies and Interests ... 58

Chapter 11: Long-Term Management of OCD ... 59

11.1 Setting Realistic Expectations ... 61

11.2 Preparing for Adolescence ... 61

11.3 Transitioning to Adult Care ... 63

Chapter 12: Stories of Hope and Recovery ... 65

12.1 Personal Success Stories ... 68

12.2 Lessons Learned from Families ... 68

12.3 Building a Future Full of Possibility ... 70

1

Understanding OCD in Young Boys

1.1 Introduction to Obsessive Compulsive Disorder

The journey into understanding Obsessive Compulsive Disorder (OCD) begins with demystifying a condition that affects millions worldwide, yet often remains shrouded in misconception and stigma. OCD is a complex mental health disorder characterized by a pattern of unwanted thoughts and fears (obsessions) that lead to repetitive behaviors (compulsions). These compulsions are not performed for pleasure but as an attempt to alleviate the distress caused by obsessions. This introductory exploration aims to lay the groundwork for comprehending how OCD manifests, particularly in young boys, setting the stage for deeper insights into its unique challenges and management strategies.

OCD's impact on young males can be profound and multifaceted, influencing their emotional well-being, social interactions, and academic performance. Boys may experience obsessions as intrusive thoughts or images that are disturbing and persistent. Common themes include fear of germs or contamination, needing things symmetrical or in a perfect order, aggressive or horrific thoughts about harming themselves or others, and troubling religious or sexual thoughts. The compulsions that follow—such as excessive handwashing, arranging objects in a particular manner, repeating rituals like checking locks or appliances, and mental compulsions like praying or repeating phrases—can consume hours of their day, significantly disrupting daily life.

Understanding OCD in young boys requires recognizing the signs early on. These might include sudden changes in behavior, unexplained outbursts of anger or frustration, decline in school performance due to concentration issues or absenteeism stemming from ritualistic behaviors. It's crucial to approach these signs with empathy and curiosity rather than judgment to encourage open communication.

- Early identification is key to managing OCD effectively.
- Comprehensive treatment plans often involve cognitive-behavioral therapy (CBT), specifically exposure-response prevention (ERP), which has shown significant success in treating OCD symptoms.
- Family involvement plays a critical role in treatment success; educating parents and siblings about OCD can foster a supportive home environment.

This section serves as an essential primer on OCD's basics—its definition, symptoms, causes, and initial steps toward effective management. By understanding these foundational aspects, caregivers are better equipped to support young boys through their journey with OCD. The subsequent sections will delve deeper into specific challenges faced by boys with OCD and practical strategies for families navigating this complex condition.

1.2 Symptoms and Diagnosis in Boys

The identification and understanding of OCD symptoms in young boys are pivotal for early intervention and effective management of the disorder. Recognizing these symptoms, however, can be challenging due to the subtle or secretive nature of compulsions and obsessions in children. Boys may not always understand their experiences well enough to articulate them, or they might fear judgment, leading to underreporting of their symptoms.

OCD manifests through a variety of obsessions and compulsions that can significantly impact a boy's daily life. Obsessions are persistent, unwanted thoughts or impulses that cause distress or anxiety. For boys, these might include fears of contamination, intense worry about harm coming to themselves or loved ones, or distress over thoughts that conflict with their moral or religious beliefs. Compulsions are repetitive behaviors or mental acts that an individual feels driven to perform in response to an obsession or according to rules that must be applied rigidly. Common compulsive behaviors in boys include excessive washing and cleaning, checking things repeatedly, arranging items in a specific order, and demanding reassurances.

Diagnosing OCD in boys involves a comprehensive evaluation by a mental health professional who specializes in child psychology. The process typically includes clinical interviews with both the child and parents, psychological questionnaires, and observation of behavior. It's crucial for the diagnosis to differentiate between OCD and normal childhood rituals or developmental phases. For instance, while many children go through phases of liking things organized in a certain way or having bedtime routines, what distinguishes OCD is the intensity of these behaviors—their interference with daily functioning—and the distress they cause.

- Early detection is critical for managing OCD effectively.
- A nuanced understanding of how symptoms manifest specifically in boys can aid parents and educators in recognizing potential warning signs.
- Treatment plans often involve cognitive-behavioral therapy (CBT), particularly exposure-response

prevention (ERP), alongside family education to support the child's recovery journey.

Understanding the nuances of OCD symptoms and diagnosis in boys is essential for caregivers and professionals alike. By fostering an environment where boys feel safe to express their worries without fear of stigma, families can take significant steps towards addressing OCD effectively. This approach not only aids in early diagnosis but also ensures that interventions are tailored to meet the unique needs of each child, paving the way for better outcomes.

1.3 Causes and Manifestations

The exploration of the causes and manifestations of Obsessive-Compulsive Disorder (OCD) in young boys is crucial for understanding the complexity of this condition. While the exact cause of OCD remains unknown, a combination of genetic, neurological, behavioral, cognitive, and environmental factors are believed to contribute to its development. This multifaceted origin underscores the importance of recognizing the diverse ways in which OCD can manifest in young boys, impacting their behavior, emotions, and daily routines.

Genetic studies suggest a hereditary component to OCD, indicating that boys with family members who have OCD are at a higher risk of developing the disorder themselves. Neurological research points to differences in certain areas of the brain, including abnormal functioning of the frontal cortex and subcortical structures, which may predispose individuals to OCD. These biological underpinnings can influence how obsessions and compulsions manifest in young boys.

From a behavioral perspective, it's posited that certain behaviors become compulsions when they are reinforced by the relief they provide from anxiety caused by obsessions. Cognitive theories suggest that boys with OCD may possess a heightened sense of responsibility and an overestimation of threat, leading them to engage in compulsive behaviors as a form of prevention against perceived dangers.

Environmental factors such as stressful life events or changes—such as moving to a new school or the birth of a sibling—can also trigger or exacerbate OCD symptoms in children who may already be predisposed to the disorder. Additionally, parenting styles that are either overly protective or critical can contribute to the development or severity of OCD symptoms by influencing how boys cope with anxiety and stress.

- Understanding these causes is vital for identifying potential risk factors early on.
- Awareness among parents and educators about these diverse influences can facilitate early intervention strategies.
- Tailoring treatment approaches to address not only the symptoms but also underlying causes is essential for effective management.

In conclusion, while there is no single cause for OCD in young boys, an interplay between genetic predisposition and environmental factors plays a significant role. Recognizing how these elements manifest uniquely in each child is key to providing targeted support and interventions that address both the symptoms and root causes of OCD.

References:

- American Psychiatric Association. (2013). Diagnostic and Statistical Manual of Mental Disorders (5th ed.). Arlington, VA: American Psychiatric Publishing.

- Pauls, D. L. (2008). The genetics of obsessive-compulsive disorder: A review of the evidence. American Journal of Medical Genetics Part C: Seminars in Medical Genetics, 148C(2), 133-139.

- Saxena, S., Rauch, S. L. (2000). Functional neuroimaging and the neuroanatomy of obsessive-compulsive disorder. Psychiatric Clinics of North America, 23(3), 563-586.

- Storch, E. A., Lewin, A. B., De Nadai, A. S., Murphy, T. K. (2010). Defining treatment response and remission in obsessive-compulsive disorder: a signal detection analysis of the Children's Yale-Brown Obsessive Compulsive Scale. Journal of the American Academy of Child & Adolescent Psychiatry, 49(7), 708-717.

- Thomsen, P. H. (2013). Obsessive-compulsive disorder in children and adolescents: Symptom dimensions in a naturalistic setting. Nordic Journal of Psychiatry, 67(5), 335-342.

2

The Impact of OCD on Daily Life

2.1 Emotional Well-being and Social Interactions

The emotional well-being and social interactions of young boys with Obsessive Compulsive Disorder (OCD) are profoundly impacted by the condition, influencing their daily lives in significant ways. This section delves into the complexities surrounding how OCD affects these critical areas, offering insights into the challenges faced and strategies for support. The importance of understanding and addressing these impacts cannot be overstated, as they play a pivotal role in the overall development and quality of life for those affected.

OCD can lead to intense feelings of anxiety, frustration, and shame in young boys, stemming from their intrusive thoughts or compulsions. These emotions can be overwhelming, often leading to a sense of isolation or misunderstanding among their peers. The fear of stigma or being perceived as different can discourage boys from engaging in social activities or sharing their experiences with others, further exacerbating feelings of loneliness.

In addition to internal struggles, external reactions from peers and adults can significantly affect a young boy's self-esteem and social interactions. Misunderstandings about OCD may lead to bullying or exclusion from group activities, which not only hinders social development but also reinforces negative self-perceptions. It is crucial for parents, caregivers, and educators to foster an environment of acceptance and understanding around mental health issues to combat these challenges.

- Encouraging open communication about feelings and experiences related to OCD.
- Providing education to peers about OCD to promote empathy and understanding.
- Implementing structured social skills training programs designed for children with OCD.

Strategies such as cognitive-behavioral therapy (CBT) have been shown to be effective not only in managing the symptoms of OCD but also in improving emotional regulation and social skills. By learning coping mechanisms through CBT or similar therapies, young boys can gain confidence in navigating social situations despite their OCD symptoms. Additionally, participation in support groups specifically tailored for children with OCD can offer a sense of community and belonging that combats feelings of isolation.

In conclusion, while OCD poses significant challenges to the emotional well-being and social interactions of young boys, understanding these impacts is the first step towards providing effective support. Through compassionate care, targeted interventions, and fostering inclusive environments both at home and school, it is possible to mitigate these effects and help boys with OCD build fulfilling relationships and lead happier lives.

2.2 Challenges in Thoughts and Behaviors

The intricate nature of Obsessive-Compulsive Disorder (OCD) extends far beyond the surface-level understanding of repeated actions or persistent thoughts. At its core, OCD profoundly disrupts the cognitive and behavioral patterns of individuals, presenting a complex web of challenges that can significantly hinder daily functioning. This section delves into the nuanced difficulties faced by those with OCD in managing their thoughts and behaviors, shedding light on the pervasive impact of this condition.

OCD is characterized by two main components: obsessions, which are unwanted and intrusive thoughts causing distress, and compulsions, which are behaviors performed in an attempt to alleviate this distress or prevent feared outcomes. The cyclical nature of obsessions leading to compulsions creates a pattern that can be incredibly hard to break. Individuals may find themselves trapped in a loop, where the completion of one compulsion only momentarily eases anxiety before another obsession takes hold.

This relentless cycle can lead to significant disruptions in daily life. For instance, someone with contamination fears might avoid public spaces or require hours to complete cleaning rituals, severely impacting their ability to engage in work or social activities. Similarly, individuals with checking compulsions may find it difficult to leave their homes due to the need to repeatedly ensure that doors are locked or appliances are turned off.

Beyond these visible manifestations, OCD also challenges individuals on a cognitive level. The constant barrage of intrusive thoughts can be mentally exhausting, leading to difficulties concentrating on tasks or making decisions. The fear of acting on harmful obsessions can cause intense anxiety and self-doubt, further complicating everyday interactions and responsibilities.

- Engaging in Exposure Response Prevention (ERP), a form of therapy specifically designed for OCD that helps individuals gradually face their fears without performing compulsions.
- Developing mindfulness techniques to increase awareness and acceptance of intrusive thoughts without engaging with them.
- Creating structured routines that provide stability and reduce opportunities for compulsive behaviors.

In conclusion, the challenges in thoughts and behaviors associated with OCD extend well beyond simple habits or quirks; they represent profound obstacles that affect every aspect of an individual's life. Understanding these complexities is crucial for developing effective treatment strategies that address both the symptoms and the underlying cognitive distortions driving them. Through targeted interventions and support, it is possible for those affected by OCD to regain control over their thoughts and actions, leading to improved functioning and quality of life.

2.3 The Role of Family and School

The influence of family and school environments on individuals with Obsessive-Compulsive Disorder (OCD) is profound, shaping not only the management and understanding of the condition but also affecting the individual's daily experiences and coping mechanisms. These social structures play pivotal roles in either facilitating a supportive atmosphere for managing OCD or inadvertently contributing to the challenges faced by those affected.

Family dynamics can significantly impact an individual's experience with OCD. A supportive family environment that promotes understanding, acceptance, and encouragement can be instrumental in helping someone manage their symptoms effectively. Education about OCD within the family unit is crucial; without a clear understanding of the disorder, family members may misinterpret symptoms as mere quirks or deliberate behaviors, potentially leading to frustration or conflict. On the other hand, families informed about OCD can provide invaluable support through empathy, patience, and assistance in seeking professional help when necessary.

School settings also play a critical role in the life of someone with OCD. Schools are not just academic institutions; they are social environments where young individuals spend a significant portion of their day. A lack of awareness about OCD among teachers and peers can lead to misunderstandings, stigmatization, and isolation. Educators equipped with knowledge about OCD can foster an inclusive environment that accommodates students' needs without singling them out or making them feel uncomfortable. Simple adjustments in teaching methods or examination protocols can make a substantial difference in helping students with OCD perform to their potential without undue stress.

Moreover, both family and school environments can act as sources of stress or triggers for OCD symptoms if not properly managed. High expectations, pressure to excel academically, or turbulent family relationships can exacerbate symptoms. Conversely, these environments can also serve as platforms for practicing therapeutic strategies learned in treatment, such as Exposure Response Prevention (ERP). For instance, homework assignments might be used as opportunities for exposure tasks under controlled conditions at home or school.

- Creating open lines of communication within families about feelings and challenges related to OCD.
- Implementing educational programs in schools to raise awareness about mental health issues including OCD.
- Encouraging collaboration between therapists, families, and schools to create consistent support networks for individuals with OCD.

In conclusion, while the challenges presented by thoughts and behaviors associated with OCD are significant on their own, the role of family and school cannot be underestimated. These environments offer unique opportunities for support and accommodation that can greatly enhance quality of life and functional outcomes for those living with OCD.

References:

- American Psychiatric Association. (2013). Diagnostic and Statistical Manual of Mental Disorders (5th ed.). Arlington, VA: American Psychiatric Publishing.

- Storch, E. A., & Lewin, A. B. (Eds.). (2014). Clinical Handbook of Obsessive-Compulsive Disorder and Related Problems. Johns Hopkins University Press.

- Foa, E. B., Yadin, E., & Lichner, T. K. (2012). Exposure and Response (Ritual) Prevention for Obsessive Compulsive Disorder: Therapist Guide (2nd ed.). Oxford University Press.

- National Institute of Mental Health. (2020). Obsessive-Compulsive Disorder: When Unwanted Thoughts or Irresistible Actions Take Over. Retrieved from https://www.nimh.nih.gov/health/topics/obsessive-compulsive-disorder-ocd

- International OCD Foundation. (n.d.). What is OCD? Retrieved from https://iocdf.org/about-ocd/

3

Building a Supportive Home Environment

3.1 Fostering Resilience and Positive Coping Mechanisms

The importance of fostering resilience and positive coping mechanisms in young boys with Obsessive Compulsive Disorder (OCD) cannot be overstated. This critical aspect of support helps children navigate the challenges posed by OCD, enabling them to develop strength and adaptability in the face of adversity. By cultivating a supportive home environment that emphasizes these qualities, caregivers can significantly impact their child's ability to manage OCD symptoms effectively.

Resilience, or the capacity to recover quickly from difficulties, is a powerful tool for anyone, but especially for those dealing with mental health challenges like OCD. It involves developing a mindset that is focused on growth and learning from experiences rather than being overwhelmed by them. For young boys with OCD, resilience can transform how they view their disorder—from a limiting factor in their lives to something they can manage and overcome.

Positive coping mechanisms are strategies that individuals use to deal with stressors in a healthy and productive way. These mechanisms are particularly vital for young boys with OCD as they navigate complex emotions and situations triggered by their symptoms. Effective coping strategies may include:

- Engaging in physical activities or hobbies that provide an outlet for stress
- Practicing mindfulness and relaxation techniques to reduce anxiety
- Utilizing cognitive-behavioral techniques to challenge and change negative thought patterns
- Seeking social support from family members, friends, or support groups who understand their experiences

To foster resilience and positive coping mechanisms at home, caregivers must create an environment where open communication is encouraged, emotional expression is supported, and achievements are celebrated. This involves not only providing practical tools and strategies for managing OCD but also modeling resilient behaviors through one's own actions.

Educating family members about OCD is another crucial step in building a supportive environment. Understanding the disorder helps demystify the child's experiences and fosters empathy within the family unit. Additionally, involving children in decisions related to their treatment plan empowers them and reinforces their sense of control over their lives.

In conclusion, fostering resilience and positive coping mechanisms within a supportive home environment plays an indispensable role in helping young boys with OCD thrive. By emphasizing these elements, caregivers equip children with the skills needed to face challenges head-on, leading to improved mental health outcomes and overall well-being.

3.2 Communication Strategies for Parents and Caregivers

The cornerstone of building a supportive home environment for young boys with Obsessive Compulsive Disorder (OCD) lies in effective communication strategies. These strategies are pivotal not only in understanding the child's needs but also in fostering an atmosphere of trust and openness. Effective communication between parents, caregivers, and children can significantly ease the stress associated with OCD, creating a more resilient and positive coping environment.

One key aspect of these communication strategies is active listening. This involves giving full attention to the child when they speak, acknowledging their feelings without immediate judgment or dismissal, and responding thoughtfully. Active listening demonstrates to the child that their thoughts and feelings are valid and important, encouraging them to share more openly.

Another vital strategy is the use of clear and positive language. This means avoiding negative labels or language that could exacerbate the child's anxieties or feelings of isolation. Instead, focusing on strengths-based language that highlights the child's abilities and efforts can boost their self-esteem and motivation to engage in coping mechanisms.

- Encouraging open dialogue about emotions by setting aside regular times for conversations, ensuring the child knows there is always an opportunity to talk.
- Using age-appropriate explanations to discuss OCD, its effects, and how it does not define the person.
- Modeling healthy communication by sharing one's own feelings and coping strategies in challenging situations.
- Reinforcing positive behavior changes or successful management of OCD symptoms through praise and recognition.

Incorporating these strategies into daily interactions requires patience and consistency from parents and caregivers. It may also involve seeking external support from therapists or counselors who can provide additional tools for enhancing communication skills within the family unit. By prioritizing effective communication, families can create a nurturing environment that empowers young boys with OCD to express themselves freely, seek support when needed, and develop healthier coping mechanisms for managing their disorder.

Beyond individual conversations, establishing a family culture where all members are encouraged to communicate openly about their mental health fosters mutual understanding and empathy. This collective approach helps demystify OCD within the family context, reducing stigma and promoting a unified front in supporting the child's journey towards managing their symptoms effectively.

3.3 Creating Routine and Structure

The establishment of routine and structure is a fundamental aspect of creating a supportive home environment, particularly for young boys with Obsessive Compulsive Disorder (OCD). This approach not only aids in managing the symptoms of OCD but also instills a sense of security and predictability, which can significantly reduce stress and anxiety levels in children. By integrating structured routines into daily life, parents and caregivers can provide a framework that helps these young individuals navigate their day-to-day activities more effectively.

Routine and structure are beneficial because they create an environment where expectations are clear, and surprises are minimized. For children with OCD, unpredictability can trigger or exacerbate symptoms. Therefore, having a predictable schedule can be incredibly soothing. It's important to note that the goal is not to create a rigid environment but rather one that balances consistency with flexibility. This balance ensures that while there is a general framework for the day, there is also room to accommodate the unique needs and situations that may arise.

- Starting the day at the same time each morning helps set the tone for what's ahead, providing stability right from the beginning.
- Incorporating regular meal times fosters family bonding and ensures nutritional needs are met consistently.

- Designating specific times for homework, play, and relaxation can help manage both academic responsibilities and leisure activities without overwhelming the child.
- Establishing bedtime routines including winding down activities like reading or quiet play promotes better sleep hygiene, crucial for mental health.

In addition to daily routines, creating structured environments at home plays a critical role. Organizing living spaces so that items have designated places reduces chaos and makes it easier for children with OCD to navigate their surroundings without feeling overwhelmed. Encouraging personal responsibility through age-appropriate chores within this structured framework reinforces independence while maintaining order.

Implementing routine and structure requires patience, as adjustments may be needed to find what works best for each child. Open communication about these routines is essential; involving children in planning can empower them and make transitions smoother. Ultimately, by fostering an atmosphere of predictability and security through routine and structure, parents and caregivers equip young boys with OCD with tools to manage their symptoms more effectively while promoting overall well-being.

References:

- American Psychiatric Association. (2020). Diagnostic and Statistical Manual of Mental Disorders (5th ed.).

- March, J.S., & Benton, C.M. (2007). Treating Obsessive-Compulsive Disorder in Children and Adolescents: A Cognitive-Behavioral Approach. Guilford Press.

- Piacentini, J., & Langley, A. (2019). Cognitive-Behavioral Therapy for Children and Adolescents with Obsessive-Compulsive Disorder. Oxford University Press.

- Storch, E.A., & Lewin, A.B. (Eds.). (2011). Handbook of Child and Adolescent Obsessive-Compulsive Disorder. Routledge.

- Wagner, A.P. (2002). Up and Down the Worry Hill: A Children's Book about Obsessive-Compulsive Disorder and its Treatment. Lighthouse Press.

4

Professional Help and Collaboration

4.1 Seeking Expert Assistance

The journey of managing Obsessive Compulsive Disorder (OCD) in young boys is complex and multifaceted, necessitating a collaborative approach that includes expert assistance. The significance of seeking professional help cannot be overstated, as it provides a cornerstone for understanding, diagnosing, and effectively treating OCD. This section delves into the critical aspects of engaging with mental health professionals and how their expertise can significantly alter the trajectory of a young boy's battle with OCD.

At the outset, recognizing when to seek expert assistance is paramount. Early intervention is key in managing OCD symptoms effectively. Parents and caregivers are often the first to notice signs of OCD in children, which may include repetitive behaviors or severe anxiety about specific thoughts or fears. Once these signs are identified, consulting with a pediatrician or a mental health professional who specializes in childhood OCD becomes an essential next step.

Finding the right specialist is crucial. Not all therapists or psychiatrists have extensive experience with OCD, particularly in children. Therefore, seeking out professionals who specialize in cognitive-behavioral therapy (CBT), especially exposure-response prevention (ERP), which has been shown to be highly effective for treating OCD, is advisable. These therapies are tailored to help individuals confront their fears without performing compulsions, under the guidance of an experienced therapist.

In addition to direct treatment strategies, mental health professionals play a vital role in educating families about OCD. This education includes debunking common myths about the disorder, providing insights into how symptoms may manifest differently in boys versus girls, and offering practical advice on creating an environment that supports recovery and resilience at home and school.

- Understanding different treatment modalities: Beyond CBT and ERP, professionals might also incorporate other therapeutic approaches such as mindfulness and relaxation techniques to help manage anxiety symptoms associated with OCD.

- Navigating medication options: In some cases, medication may be recommended alongside therapy to help manage symptoms more effectively. A child psychiatrist can provide guidance on the best pharmacological options based on the individual's needs.

- Building a support network: Professionals can also guide families toward building a supportive network by connecting them with support groups, educational resources, and community services dedicated to OCD management.

Ultimately, seeking expert assistance is not just about obtaining a diagnosis or undergoing treatment; it's about empowering young boys with OCD and their families with knowledge, strategies, and hope for overcoming challenges associated with the disorder. By collaborating closely with specialists who understand the nuances of OCD in children, families can navigate this journey with greater confidence and support.

4.2 Advocating for Educational Accommodations

The process of advocating for educational accommodations is a critical step in supporting young boys with Obsessive Compulsive Disorder (OCD) within the school environment. This advocacy is essential because it ensures that these students receive the necessary modifications or supports to succeed academically and socially, despite the challenges posed by OCD. The importance of educational accommodations lies in their ability to level the playing field, providing an equitable opportunity for students with OCD to access learning and participate fully in school activities.

Advocating for accommodations often begins with understanding the specific needs of the student. This involves close collaboration between parents, educators, and mental health professionals to identify how OCD affects the student's school performance and participation. For instance, extended time on tests might be necessary for a student who struggles with compulsive rechecking, while a quiet room for exams may benefit those overwhelmed by sensory stimuli or intrusive thoughts.

Another crucial aspect of advocacy is navigating the legal framework that supports educational accommodations. In many regions, laws such as the Individuals with Disabilities Education Act (IDEA) in the United States mandate that schools provide individualized education programs (IEPs) or 504 plans to eligible students with disabilities, including those with significant OCD symptoms. Understanding these laws empowers parents and caregivers to request formal evaluations and advocate effectively for accommodations that address their child's unique needs.

- Gathering documentation from healthcare providers that outlines how OCD impacts learning and recommending specific accommodations.
- Communicating openly with school staff about the child's condition and its effects on their education.

- Ensuring ongoing dialogue between all parties involved to adjust accommodations as needed based on the student's evolving needs.

In addition to formal accommodations, fostering an inclusive school culture is paramount. Educating teachers and peers about OCD can promote understanding and reduce stigma, creating a more supportive environment for affected students. Workshops or training sessions on mental health awareness can equip school staff with strategies to support students both inside and outside of the classroom effectively.

Ultimately, advocating for educational accommodations is not just about securing specific supports but also about championing a broader understanding of OCD within educational settings. By doing so, families and educators can work together to ensure that every student has access to an education that accommodates their individual needs, allowing them to thrive academically and personally despite the challenges posed by OCD.

4.3 Working with Therapists and Medical Professionals

The collaboration between families, educators, and healthcare providers is paramount in supporting young boys with Obsessive Compulsive Disorder (OCD). This partnership is crucial for developing a comprehensive support system that addresses both the educational and health-related needs of the student. Engaging with therapists and medical professionals not only aids in managing the symptoms of OCD but also ensures that the child's academic journey is not hindered by their condition.

Working closely with therapists allows for a tailored approach to treatment that can significantly improve the quality of life for children with OCD. These professionals can offer cognitive-behavioral therapy (CBT), which is considered one of the most effective treatments for OCD. CBT focuses on changing harmful thought patterns and behaviors, providing students with strategies to cope with their compulsions and anxieties. Moreover, therapists can collaborate with school staff to implement these strategies within the educational setting, ensuring consistency in the child's management plan.

Medical professionals play a critical role in diagnosing OCD and determining the appropriate course of treatment, which may include medication alongside therapy. Medications such as selective serotonin reuptake inhibitors (SSRIs) are commonly prescribed to help manage OCD symptoms. It's essential for parents and caregivers to maintain open communication with psychiatrists or pediatricians overseeing medication plans to monitor side effects and effectiveness, adjusting dosages as necessary.

- Establishing regular meetings between parents, educators, and healthcare providers to discuss progress and make adjustments to treatment plans.
- Providing training for school staff on how to recognize signs of distress or anxiety in students with OCD and how to respond appropriately.
- Creating a supportive network that includes peer support groups where students can share experiences and coping strategies under professional guidance.

In addition to direct interventions, fostering an environment of understanding within schools through education about mental health conditions like OCD is vital. This awareness can reduce stigma, encourage empathy among peers, and promote a culture where students feel safe disclosing their struggles without fear of judgment. Ultimately, working collaboratively with therapists and medical professionals forms a cornerstone of effective support for students with OCD, enabling them to navigate both their academic paths and personal challenges more successfully.

References:

- American Psychiatric Association. (2013). Diagnostic and Statistical Manual of Mental Disorders (5th ed.). Arlington, VA: American Psychiatric Publishing.

- March, J.S., & Benton, C.M. (2007). The role of medications in the treatment of pediatric OCD. Child and Adolescent Psychiatric Clinics of North America, 16(1), 187-203.

- Piacentini, J., Bergman, R.L., Keller, M., & McCracken, J. (2003). Functional impairment in children and adolescents with obsessive-compulsive disorder. Journal of Child and Adolescent Psychopharmacology, 13(Suppl 1), S61-S69.

- Storch, E.A., Murphy, T.K., Geffken, G.R., Sajid, M., & Goodman, W.K. (2004). Cognitive-behavioral therapy for children and adolescents with obsessive-compulsive disorder: A review and recommendations for treatment. Journal of the American Academy of Child & Adolescent Psychiatry, 43(3), 331-341.

5

Empowering Young Boys with OCD

5.1 Understanding the Condition

The initial step in empowering young boys with Obsessive Compulsive Disorder (OCD) involves a comprehensive understanding of the condition itself. This foundational knowledge is crucial for parents, caregivers, and educators to effectively support and guide these young individuals through their unique challenges. OCD is characterized by a pattern of unwanted thoughts or fears (obsessions) that lead to repetitive behaviors (compulsions). These compulsions are performed in an attempt to alleviate the distress caused by the obsessions.

OCD manifests differently in every individual, making it essential to recognize how it specifically affects young boys. In many cases, their obsessions and compulsions can revolve around themes like cleanliness, symmetry, order, or fears of harm coming to themselves or loved ones. It's important to note that these behaviors go beyond typical childhood routines or superstitions; they are intense actions that significantly interfere with daily life.

Understanding the impact of OCD on young boys extends beyond recognizing symptoms. It involves acknowledging how these symptoms affect their emotional well-being, social interactions, and academic performance. Boys may feel isolated because of their compulsions or fear judgment from peers, leading to social withdrawal or difficulties in school environments where their routines are disrupted.

- Recognizing early signs of OCD in boys is critical for timely intervention.
- Understanding that OCD's manifestations can be diverse and may not always align with common stereotypes.
- Acknowledging the emotional toll and potential for increased anxiety or depression associated with OCD.

In addition to identifying symptoms and impacts, grasping the underlying causes of OCD is part of understanding the condition. While the exact cause remains unknown, a combination of genetic, neurological, behavioral, cognitive, and environmental factors are believed to contribute. This multifaceted origin underscores why personalized approaches to treatment and support are necessary.

Ultimately, deepening our comprehension of OCD in young boys paves the way for more empathetic support systems. By demystifying the disorder and promoting open dialogue about mental health from an early age, we can foster environments where boys feel safe expressing themselves and seeking help. This approach not only aids in managing OCD but also contributes to building resilience and self-understanding among affected individuals.

5.2 Communicating Experiences

The importance of communicating experiences for young boys with Obsessive Compulsive Disorder (OCD) cannot be overstated. This section delves into the nuanced ways in which these individuals can express their thoughts and feelings, thereby reducing the isolation and misunderstanding that often accompany this condition. Effective communication serves as a bridge between experiencing OCD symptoms and receiving the understanding and support needed from parents, caregivers, educators, and peers.

For many young boys with OCD, articulating the nature of their obsessions and compulsions can be daunting. The fear of not being understood or of facing judgment can silence them, exacerbating feelings of loneliness and difference. Encouraging open dialogue in a non-judgmental environment is crucial. This involves educating those around them about the disorder's complexities beyond mere stereotypes or misconceptions.

One approach to fostering communication is through structured activities that allow for expression in less direct forms, such as art therapy or storytelling. These methods can provide insights into a child's inner world without requiring them to explicitly articulate their fears or behaviors, which they may find difficult to do. Additionally, engaging in role-playing exercises can help boys develop strategies for confronting OCD-related challenges in social settings, empowering them to communicate their needs and boundaries more effectively.

- Creating safe spaces where boys feel comfortable sharing their experiences without fear of judgment or reprisal.
- Utilizing creative outlets as alternative means for expressing complex emotions and thoughts related to OCD.
- Teaching effective communication strategies tailored to individual needs, promoting self-advocacy within educational settings and personal relationships.

In conclusion, enhancing communication skills in young boys with OCD is a multifaceted endeavor that requires patience, creativity, and an inclusive approach from all involved. By prioritizing open dialogue and providing various platforms for expression, we can empower these individuals to navigate their condition with confidence and support.

Beyond individual expression, it's also beneficial to involve young boys with OCD in group discussions or support networks with peers facing similar challenges. This collective sharing can normalize their experiences, reduce stigma, and build a community of understanding and empathy. Through these shared narratives, boys learn not only how to articulate their own experiences but also gain perspective on the diverse manifestations of OCD among others.

5.3 Participating in Treatment Plans

The journey of managing Obsessive Compulsive Disorder (OCD) in young boys is significantly enhanced by active participation in their treatment plans. This engagement not only fosters a sense of ownership over their recovery process but also empowers them to confront OCD with resilience and determination. Participation in treatment planning can take various forms, from selecting therapeutic activities that resonate with them, to setting personal goals and celebrating milestones.

One critical aspect of involving young boys in their treatment plans is the collaborative establishment of achievable goals. These objectives should be specific, measurable, attainable, relevant, and time-bound (SMART). By working together with therapists and caregivers to set these goals, boys learn the value of intentionality and the satisfaction of accomplishment.

This practice encourages persistence even when faced with challenges inherent to OCD management.

Moreover, incorporating preferred interests into therapy can significantly enhance engagement. For instance, if a child has an affinity for art or music, therapists might integrate these elements into cognitive-behavioral therapy sessions. Such personalized approaches not only make therapy more enjoyable but also more effective, as they leverage intrinsic motivations and familiar contexts to tackle difficult topics.

- Encouraging self-reflection through journaling or digital apps designed for mood tracking and symptom recording.
- Involving boys in decision-making about therapeutic approaches or interventions to foster a sense of agency.
- Creating opportunities for peer interaction within therapeutic settings to build social support networks among those undergoing similar experiences.

Active participation also extends beyond formal therapy sessions. Engaging in regular discussions about feelings, progress, setbacks, and strategies for coping with OCD symptoms at home cultivates an environment where boys feel supported and understood. This ongoing dialogue ensures that treatment plans remain dynamic and responsive to the child's evolving needs.

To conclude, active involvement in treatment planning is indispensable for empowering young boys with OCD. It transforms them from passive recipients into proactive participants in their journey towards wellness. By fostering collaboration between the child, caregivers, and professionals, we lay a foundation for enduring resilience and self-efficacy in managing OCD.

References:

- American Psychiatric Association. (2013). Diagnostic and statistical manual of mental disorders (5th ed.). Arlington, VA: American Psychiatric Publishing.

- March, J. S., & Mulle, K. (1998). OCD in Children and Adolescents: A Cognitive-Behavioral Treatment Manual. New York: Guilford Press.

- Foa, E. B., Yadin, E., & Lichner, T. K. (2012). Exposure and response (ritual) prevention for obsessive-compulsive disorder: Therapist guide (2nd ed.). Oxford University Press.

- Storch, E. A., & Lewin, A. B. (Eds.). (2011). Handbook of child and adolescent obsessive-compulsive disorder. Routledge/Taylor & Francis Group.

- MindShiftâ„¢ CBT - Anxiety Canada App designed to help teens and young adults cope with anxiety by teaching them how to relax, develop more helpful ways of thinking, and identify active steps that will help them take charge of their anxiety.

6

Treatment Approaches for OCD

6.1 Cognitive-Behavioral Therapy (CBT)

Cognitive-Behavioral Therapy (CBT) stands as a cornerstone in the treatment of Obsessive-Compulsive Disorder (OCD), particularly for young boys grappling with this condition. Its significance lies not only in its evidence-based approach but also in its adaptability to cater to the unique challenges and needs of this demographic. CBT's core principle revolves around the interconnectedness of thoughts, feelings, and behaviors, offering a structured method through which individuals can identify and challenge unhelpful patterns that contribute to their OCD symptoms.

The application of CBT for young boys with OCD involves several key components, each designed to empower them towards managing their disorder effectively. One of the primary strategies is exposure and response prevention (ERP), a technique that gently exposes individuals to their feared objects or situations without allowing them to engage in their usual compulsive responses. This method helps reduce anxiety over time and teaches boys that they can cope with discomfort without resorting to compulsions.

Another critical aspect of CBT is cognitive restructuring, which encourages boys to recognize and alter distorted beliefs related to their obsessions. Through guided discovery, a therapist helps the child question the validity of these intrusive thoughts and replace them with more realistic perspectives. This process not only aids in alleviating distress but also fosters a healthier relationship with one's thought patterns.

- Building coping skills: Developing effective stress-management techniques such as relaxation exercises or mindfulness practices.
- Enhancing problem-solving abilities: Teaching young boys how to confront daily challenges related to OCD head-on, promoting resilience.

- Social skills training: Addressing any interpersonal issues stemming from OCD behaviors, thereby improving social interactions and support networks.

Incorporating family involvement is another pivotal element of CBT for young boys with OCD. Educating parents and caregivers about the disorder and involving them in treatment plans enhances the support system at home, creating an environment conducive to recovery. It allows families to understand how best to respond to OCD symptoms without reinforcing them, fostering a collaborative effort towards managing the condition.

Overall, CBT offers a comprehensive framework for treating OCD in young boys by equipping them with practical tools and strategies tailored to their specific experiences. Its effectiveness is amplified when combined with ongoing support from therapists, educators, and family members alike, ensuring that each boy has the resources needed to navigate his journey toward well-being confidently.

6.2 Exposure-Response Prevention (ERP)

Exposure-Response Prevention (ERP) is a critical component of Cognitive-Behavioral Therapy (CBT) for treating Obsessive-Compulsive Disorder (OCD), particularly effective in breaking the cycle of obsessive thoughts and compulsive behaviors. This technique involves the deliberate exposure of the patient to the sources of their anxiety or obsessions without allowing them to perform their usual compulsive responses. The fundamental principle behind ERP is that through repeated exposures, the individual learns to tolerate the discomfort and anxiety associated with their obsessions, leading to a gradual decrease in their OCD symptoms.

The process of ERP begins with the therapist working closely with the patient to create a hierarchy of feared situations, starting from those that provoke minimal anxiety and gradually moving up to more distressing scenarios. This structured approach allows individuals to face their fears in a controlled and manageable way, ensuring they do not become overwhelmed by anxiety. During these exposure exercises, patients are encouraged to resist the urge to engage in compulsions, thereby learning that anxiety naturally decreases over time even without performing these rituals.

A key aspect of ERP's effectiveness lies in its ability to challenge and modify the beliefs underlying OCD symptoms. Patients often hold certain catastrophic beliefs about what might happen if they do not perform their compulsions. Through repeated exposures where nothing bad happens despite not engaging in compulsive behaviors, these beliefs are gradually disconfirmed. This cognitive shift is crucial for long-term improvement and helps reduce both the intensity and frequency of OCD symptoms.

- Building tolerance: Gradually increasing exposure levels helps build tolerance towards anxiety-provoking stimuli.
- Reducing avoidance: By confronting feared objects or situations directly, patients learn that avoidance is not necessary for managing anxiety.
- Enhancing self-efficacy: Successfully resisting compulsions boosts confidence in one's ability to cope with anxiety without resorting to OCD behaviors.

Incorporating ERP into treatment plans requires careful consideration and customization according to each patient's specific needs and thresholds for anxiety. It is often accompanied by other therapeutic interventions such as cognitive restructuring, which aids in addressing distorted thought patterns associated with OCD. Moreover, involving family members or caregivers in understanding and supporting ERP practices can enhance treatment outcomes by providing a supportive environment conducive to recovery.

Overall, ERP stands as a testament to the adaptability and efficacy of CBT approaches in treating OCD. By directly targeting the mechanisms that sustain obsessive-compulsive cycles, ERP offers individuals a path towards reclaiming control over their thoughts and actions, ultimately leading towards improved mental health and quality of life.

6.3 Mindfulness and Relaxation Exercises

Mindfulness and relaxation exercises serve as vital components in the treatment of Obsessive-Compulsive Disorder (OCD), complementing more direct approaches like Exposure-Response Prevention (ERP).

These techniques focus on reducing the overall anxiety levels and improving the capacity to tolerate distressing thoughts without resorting to compulsive behaviors. The essence of mindfulness is to bring the individual's attention to the present moment, fostering an attitude of acceptance towards their experiences, including uncomfortable thoughts and feelings.

The practice of mindfulness for OCD involves observing one's thoughts and sensations without judgment or immediate reaction. This approach helps individuals recognize that thoughts are transient and do not necessarily require a compulsive response. By cultivating a non-reactive stance, patients learn to detach from obsessive thoughts, viewing them as mere products of their mind that do not hold intrinsic power or truth.

Relaxation exercises, such as deep breathing, progressive muscle relaxation, and guided imagery, are employed to lower the body's stress response associated with OCD symptoms. These practices can be particularly beneficial before or during exposure exercises, as they equip individuals with tools to manage anxiety in real-time. For instance, deep breathing techniques can help mitigate the physiological arousal triggered by exposure to feared stimuli, making it easier for patients to remain engaged with the ERP process without becoming overwhelmed.

- Enhancing mindfulness skills: Regular meditation or mindfulness-based activities increase awareness and acceptance of present-moment experiences.
- Applying relaxation strategies: Techniques like deep breathing or progressive muscle relaxation offer immediate relief from acute stress and facilitate a calmer state of mind.
- Integrating practices into daily life: Encouraging patients to incorporate mindfulness and relaxation exercises into their daily routines ensures these tools are readily available when OCD symptoms arise.

Incorporating mindfulness and relaxation exercises into treatment plans for OCD offers a holistic approach that addresses both the cognitive aspects of obsessions and compulsions as well as the physiological underpinnings of anxiety. By learning to observe their internal experiences with curiosity rather than fear, individuals can disrupt the cycle of OCD. Moreover, these practices promote general well-being and resilience against stress, contributing positively to overall mental health beyond the scope of OCD symptoms alone.

Ultimately, while ERP targets the behavioral patterns maintaining OCD directly, mindfulness and relaxation exercises enhance this process by improving emotional regulation and stress management capabilities. Together, these strategies form a comprehensive treatment framework that addresses multiple dimensions of OCD—cognitive, behavioral, and physiological—offering individuals a robust set of skills for managing their symptoms effectively.

References:

- Didonna, F. (Ed.). (2009). Clinical Handbook of Mindfulness. Springer. This handbook provides a comprehensive overview of mindfulness interventions in clinical practice, including its application for OCD.

- Hayes, S. C., Strosahl, K., & Wilson, K. G. (2012). Acceptance and Commitment Therapy: The Process and Practice of Mindful Change. Guilford Press. This book introduces Acceptance and Commitment Therapy

(ACT), which incorporates mindfulness strategies to help individuals live better with their thoughts.

- Hofmann, S. G., Asmundson, G. J., & Beck, A. T. (2013). The Science of Cognitive Behavioral Therapy. Academic Press. It discusses the scientific underpinnings of CBT and includes sections on how mindfulness and relaxation techniques can be integrated into treatment for anxiety disorders like OCD.

- Marchand, W. R. (2012). Mindfulness-Based Stress Reduction, Mindfulness-Based Cognitive Therapy, and Zen Meditation for Depression, Anxiety, Pain, and Psychological Distress. Journal of Psychiatric PracticeÂ®, 18(4), 233-252.This article reviews evidence on the effectiveness of mindfulness practices for various psychological conditions.

7

Addressing Misconceptions and Stigma

7.1 Debunking Common Myths about OCD

The importance of addressing and debunking common myths about Obsessive-Compulsive Disorder (OCD) cannot be overstated, especially when considering its impact on young boys. Misconceptions about OCD can lead to stigma, misunderstanding, and isolation for those affected by the disorder. By challenging these myths, we foster a more informed and compassionate environment that encourages individuals to seek help and support.

One prevalent myth is that OCD is just about being overly tidy or afraid of germs. This oversimplification ignores the vast spectrum of obsessions and compulsions experienced by individuals with OCD. For young boys, their symptoms might manifest in less recognized forms such as intrusive thoughts, an overwhelming need for symmetry, or even hoarding behaviors.

Another common misconception is that people with OCD can simply 'stop thinking about it' or control their compulsions if they really want to. This belief undermines the complex nature of OCD, which is a neurobiological condition that requires professional treatment. Techniques like Cognitive Behavioral Therapy (CBT) and Exposure Response Prevention (ERP) are often necessary to manage symptoms effectively.

- OCD is not limited to cleanliness or orderliness; it encompasses a wide range of obsessions and compulsions.
- OCD cannot be overcome through willpower alone; it's a serious mental health condition that necessitates professional intervention.
- Children with OCD are not acting out or seeking attention; their behaviors are manifestations of their disorder.

Furthermore, there's a myth suggesting that children with OCD are just going through a phase or seeking attention. This misconception can lead to delays in diagnosis and treatment, exacerbating the child's distress and potentially leading to more severe symptoms over time. Recognizing OCD as a legitimate mental health issue is crucial in providing timely and effective support for young boys grappling with this disorder.

In conclusion, debunking myths surrounding OCD is vital in changing perceptions and reducing stigma associated with this condition. By educating parents, caregivers, educators, and the broader community about the realities of OCD—especially as it presents in young boys—we pave the way for greater understanding, empathy, and support for those affected by this challenging disorder.

7.2 Challenging Societal Stigmas

The endeavor to challenge societal stigmas surrounding mental health disorders, particularly OCD, is a critical step towards fostering a more inclusive and understanding society. Stigma not only exacerbates the struggles of those dealing with OCD but also significantly hampers their willingness to seek help and discuss their experiences openly. By confronting these stigmas head-on, communities can create environments where individuals feel supported and acknowledged, rather than marginalized.

One effective strategy in challenging societal stigmas is through education and awareness campaigns that aim to dispel myths and provide accurate information about OCD. These campaigns can take various forms, including workshops, seminars, social media initiatives, and public speaking events. By educating the public on the complexities of OCD, its symptoms, and the challenges faced by those who live with it, we can begin to dismantle misconceptions that contribute to stigma.

Another crucial approach involves amplifying the voices of those directly affected by OCD. Personal stories and testimonials can be powerful tools in humanizing the disorder, offering real-life insights into the struggles and triumphs of individuals living with OCD. These narratives can foster empathy and understanding among the broader public, making it harder for stigmatizing attitudes to persist.

- Education plays a pivotal role in changing perceptions about OCD by debunking myths and spreading factual information.
- Personal stories from individuals with OCD can demystify the disorder and promote empathy.
- Support groups and advocacy organizations are vital in providing platforms for shared experiences and collective action against stigma.

In addition to these efforts, support from mental health professionals is indispensable in challenging societal stigmas. Professionals can offer authoritative insights into OCD, advocate for evidence-based treatments, and push back against harmful stereotypes. Furthermore, they play a significant role in guiding families on how to support their loved ones without inadvertently reinforcing stigma.

In conclusion, challenging societal stigmas around OCD requires a multifaceted approach that includes education, personal storytelling, professional advocacy, and community support. Through concerted efforts across these domains, it is possible to cultivate an environment where individuals with OCD feel empowered to seek help without fear of judgment or discrimination.

7.3 Promoting Open Dialogue about Mental Health

The promotion of open dialogue about mental health is a pivotal step in the journey towards destigmatization and creating a supportive environment for individuals with conditions like OCD. This initiative not only complements efforts to challenge societal stigmas but also serves as a foundational element in building understanding, empathy, and actionable support within communities. Encouraging conversations around mental health issues can significantly reduce the isolation and misunderstanding that many individuals face, fostering a culture of acceptance and help-seeking behavior.

Open dialogue involves various strategies aimed at normalizing mental health discussions, both in personal settings and public forums. Educational institutions, workplaces, and media platforms play crucial roles in facilitating these conversations. By integrating mental health education into school curricula and providing training for employees, we can create informed communities that approach mental health with sensitivity and knowledge.

- Implementing mental health awareness programs in schools to educate students from an early age.
- Creating policies in workplaces that encourage employees to speak openly about their mental health challenges without fear of repercussion.
- Utilizing social media and other digital platforms to share information, personal stories, and support resources widely.

Beyond institutional efforts, the empowerment of individuals to share their experiences plays a critical role in promoting open dialogue. When people feel safe to discuss their struggles with OCD or other mental health conditions openly, it not only aids their own recovery process but also helps others to understand the multifaceted nature of these disorders. Peer-led initiatives such as support groups or online forums offer valuable spaces where individuals can connect over shared experiences, offering insights into coping mechanisms, treatment options, and mutual encouragement.

In conclusion, promoting open dialogue about mental health requires concerted efforts across multiple sectors of society. By fostering environments where talking about mental health is encouraged and supported, we can dismantle barriers to seeking help and contribute to a more inclusive community. This approach not only aids those directly affected by conditions like OCD but also educates the broader public on the importance of mental wellness.

References:

- Clement, S., Schauman, O., Graham, T., Maggioni, F., Evans-Lacko, S., Bezborodovs, N., ... & Thornicroft, G. (2015). What is the impact of mental health-related stigma on help-seeking? A systematic review of quantitative and qualitative studies. Psychological Medicine, 45(1), 11-27.

- Gulliver, A., Griffiths, K. M., & Christensen, H. (2010). Perceived barriers and facilitators to mental health help-seeking in young people: a systematic review. BMC Psychiatry, 10(1), 113.

- Kitchener, B. A., & Jorm, A. F. (2002). Mental health first aid training for the public: Evaluation of effects on knowledge, attitudes and helping behavior. BMC Psychiatry, 2(1), 10.

- Rickwood D., Dean F.M., Wilson C.J. (2007). When and how do young people seek professional help for mental health problems? Medical Journal of Australia, 187(S7), S35-S39.
- Corrigan P.W., Druss B.G., Perlick D.A. (2014). The Impact of Mental Illness Stigma on Seeking and Participating in Mental Health Care. Psychological Science in the Public Interest, 15(2), 37-70.

8

Community Resources and Support

8.1 Finding Support Groups

Finding the right support groups for families navigating Obsessive Compulsive Disorder (OCD) in young boys is a critical step towards understanding and managing this condition effectively. Support groups offer a unique platform where parents, caregivers, and educators can share experiences, strategies, and encouragement with others facing similar challenges. This collective wisdom not only provides emotional solace but also equips members with practical tools to help their children thrive despite the hurdles posed by OCD.

The journey to finding suitable support groups may begin within local communities. Many hospitals, mental health clinics, and community centers host regular meetings for families affected by various conditions, including OCD. These gatherings are often facilitated by professionals who can provide expert insights alongside peer support. Additionally, educational institutions may have resources or connections to support networks that cater specifically to students dealing with mental health issues.

In the digital age, online forums and social media platforms have emerged as invaluable resources for finding support groups. Websites dedicated to mental health awareness often host forums where individuals from around the globe can connect, share stories, and offer advice. Social media groups focused on OCD in children create safe spaces for parents and caregivers to seek guidance and reassurance from those in similar situations.

When selecting a support group, it's important to consider the group's focus—whether it's primarily on sharing emotional experiences or if it also includes educational components like guest speakers or therapy techniques. A well-rounded group that matches a family's needs can significantly impact their ability to manage OCD symptoms effectively.

Engaging in these communities fosters a sense of belonging and hope, reminding families they are not alone in their journey toward healing and resilience.

- Local Mental Health Clinics: Often offer family support sessions or can direct you to nearby groups.
- Educational Institutions: Schools may have partnerships with mental health organizations that run support groups for students and their families.
- Online Forums: Platforms like Reddit or specialized mental health websites provide subforums dedicated to OCD discussions.
- Social Media Groups: Facebook, Instagram, and other social networks have numerous private groups where members share resources and experiences related to raising children with OCD.

8.2 Utilizing Online Forums

In the digital landscape, online forums have become a cornerstone for those seeking support in managing Obsessive Compulsive Disorder (OCD) among young boys. These platforms offer an expansive network of resources, advice, and shared experiences that can significantly alleviate the sense of isolation families may feel. The value of these forums lies not only in their accessibility but also in the diversity of perspectives and strategies they encompass.

Online forums cater to a wide range of needs and preferences, making them a versatile tool for families navigating OCD. They provide an anonymous space where individuals can freely express concerns, share successes, and seek guidance without fear of judgment. This anonymity encourages open communication and fosters a supportive community environment where members feel understood and supported.

The interactive nature of online forums allows for real-time exchange of information and immediate support. Whether it's discussing therapy options, medication effects, or daily coping mechanisms, these platforms facilitate a dynamic flow of knowledge. Moreover, many forums are moderated by professionals who contribute expert advice and ensure discussions remain constructive and informative.

- Global Connectivity: Users can connect with others from different geographical locations, broadening their understanding of OCD management across cultures.

- 24/7 Availability: Unlike scheduled meetings or appointments, online forums provide round-the-clock access to support.
- Variety of Perspectives: The diverse membership offers multiple viewpoints on treatment modalities, educational strategies, and lifestyle adjustments.
- Resource Sharing: Members often share links to articles, research studies, and other educational materials that can enhance understanding and advocacy efforts.

Engaging with online forums also empowers families to become advocates for their children's well-being. By learning from others' experiences and sharing their own journeys, parents and caregivers can develop a more nuanced approach to managing OCD. This collective wisdom not only enriches the individual family's strategy but also contributes to the broader community's knowledge base.

In conclusion, utilizing online forums is an invaluable strategy for families dealing with OCD in young boys. These platforms offer emotional support, practical advice, and a sense of community that can significantly impact their ability to navigate the challenges posed by OCD. As part of a comprehensive support system that includes professional guidance and local resources, online forums play a crucial role in fostering resilience and hope among affected families.

8.3 Educational Workshops for Families

The significance of educational workshops for families, especially those navigating the complexities of Obsessive Compulsive Disorder (OCD) in young boys, cannot be overstated. These workshops serve as a vital bridge between clinical support and day-to-day management strategies for OCD. By participating in these sessions, families gain not only knowledge but also the confidence to apply practical solutions within their home environments.

Educational workshops are designed to address a broad spectrum of topics relevant to OCD and its impact on family dynamics. They range from understanding the basics of OCD, recognizing symptoms, and learning about the latest treatment options, to managing school-related issues and advocating for accommodations. The interactive nature of these workshops encourages participants to ask questions, share experiences, and seek personalized advice.

- Comprehensive Understanding: Workshops provide a deep dive into what OCD is and how it affects individuals differently. This foundational knowledge is crucial for families to identify specific challenges they might face.
- Strategies for Home Management: Practical advice on creating an OCD-friendly home environment helps in reducing stressors that can trigger or exacerbate symptoms.
- Navigating Educational Systems: Guidance on how to work with schools to ensure children receive the necessary support while maintaining their academic progress.
- Building Support Networks: Opportunities to connect with other families facing similar challenges, fostering a sense of community and shared resilience.

Beyond providing information, these workshops empower families by highlighting success stories and coping mechanisms that have worked for others. Facilitators often include mental health professionals who bring clinical insights into everyday language, making complex concepts more accessible. Additionally, many workshops incorporate activities designed to strengthen family bonds and improve communication skills, which are essential when supporting a child with OCD.

In conclusion, educational workshops offer a multifaceted approach to supporting families dealing with OCD. They not only equip participants with knowledge but also foster an environment of empathy and understanding. As part of a holistic support system that includes professional therapy and community resources like online forums, these workshops play an indispensable role in enhancing the well-being of both individuals with OCD and their families.

References:

- American Psychiatric Association. (n.d.). What Is Obsessive-Compulsive Disorder? Retrieved from https://www.psychiatry.org/patients-families/ocd/what-is-obsessive-compulsive-disorder

- International OCD Foundation. (n.d.). OCD in Kids. Retrieved from https://iocdf.org/about-ocd/ocd-in-kids/

- Anxiety and Depression Association of America. (n.d.). Understanding the Facts: Obsessive-Compulsive Disorder (OCD). Retrieved from https://adaa.org/understanding-anxiety/obsessive-compulsive-disorder-ocd

- Child Mind Institute. (n.d.). OCD: What Parents Should Know. Retrieved from https://childmind.org/guide/parents-guide-to-ocd/

- National Institute of Mental Health. (n.d.). Obsessive-Compulsive Disorder: When Unwanted Thoughts or Repetitive Behaviors Take Over. Retrieved from https://www.nimh.nih.gov/health/topics/obsessive-compulsive-disorder-ocd

9

Navigating School Life

9.1 Collaborating with Educators

The journey of navigating school life for young boys with Obsessive Compulsive Disorder (OCD) is significantly influenced by the collaboration between parents or caregivers and educators. This partnership is pivotal in creating a supportive educational environment that accommodates the unique needs of these students, fostering their academic and social development. The essence of this collaboration lies in mutual understanding, communication, and shared strategies aimed at empowering the child to thrive despite the challenges posed by OCD.

Effective collaboration begins with open and honest communication about the child's condition, ensuring that educators are fully aware of the specific manifestations of OCD in the student. This knowledge equips teachers with the insight needed to recognize behaviors or situations that may trigger anxiety or compulsions in the child. Furthermore, it enables educators to differentiate between typical childhood behaviors and those influenced by OCD, allowing for more empathetic and supportive responses.

- Developing Individualized Education Plans (IEPs) or 504 plans tailored to meet the specific needs of students with OCD.
- Implementing classroom accommodations such as extended time for assignments, alternative testing environments, or permission to leave the classroom when necessary.
- Training for school staff on OCD awareness to foster a supportive school culture.
- Regular meetings between parents/caregivers and educators to discuss progress, challenges, and adjustments to strategies or accommodations as needed.

In addition to these practical steps, fostering an inclusive classroom environment is crucial. Educators can play a significant role in challenging misconceptions about OCD among peers by promoting understanding and empathy. Activities that encourage peer support can demystify mental health conditions, reducing stigma and facilitating a more accepting social environment for all students.

The collaborative efforts between families and educators not only support academic success but also contribute significantly to the emotional well-being of young boys with OCD. By working together, they can create a nurturing educational experience that recognizes each child's potential beyond their disorder, encouraging resilience and self-confidence. Ultimately, this collaborative approach lays a foundation for positive school experiences that contribute to lifelong learning and personal growth.

9.2 Implementing Individualized Education Plans (IEPs)

The implementation of Individualized Education Plans (IEPs) is a critical step in ensuring that students with Obsessive Compulsive Disorder (OCD) receive the tailored educational support they need to succeed academically and socially. IEPs are legally binding documents developed by a team, including educators, parents or caregivers, and often the student themselves, outlining specific accommodations, supports, and goals tailored to the student's unique needs. This process is central to creating an inclusive educational environment where students with OCD can thrive.

Implementing an IEP begins with a comprehensive evaluation of the student's strengths, challenges, and specific manifestations of OCD. This assessment informs the development of personalized learning objectives and the selection of appropriate accommodations such as modified homework assignments, testing environments, or behavioral support strategies. For instance, a student might be given additional time for tests or assignments to alleviate pressure and reduce anxiety triggers associated with time constraints.

- Collaborative meetings to review and adjust the IEP based on the student's evolving needs and progress.
- Professional development for educators on OCD-specific strategies to ensure they are equipped to provide effective support.

- Regular communication between all members of the IEP team, including parents or caregivers, to share insights and observations from both home and school contexts.

Beyond academic accommodations, implementing an IEP also involves social-emotional support tailored to help students navigate interpersonal relationships and school culture. Activities designed to foster peer understanding and empathy can be included in the plan, promoting a supportive classroom environment that discourages stigma and isolation. Moreover, access to school-based mental health services can be arranged as part of the IEP to provide ongoing emotional support and coping strategies for managing OCD symptoms.

In essence, effectively implementing an IEP requires a dynamic approach that adapts over time to meet the changing needs of the student. It is not merely about academic adjustments but encompasses a holistic strategy aimed at supporting the overall well-being of students with OCD. Through this individualized approach, educators can empower these students not only to achieve their academic goals but also to build resilience and self-confidence that will serve them throughout their lives.

9.3 Social Integration Strategies

The importance of social integration for students with Obsessive Compulsive Disorder (OCD) cannot be overstated. While Individualized Education Plans (IEPs) primarily focus on academic accommodations and supports, they also play a crucial role in facilitating the social integration of these students. This section delves into strategies that can be employed to ensure students with OCD are not only included but actively integrated into the social fabric of the school community.

Creating an inclusive environment goes beyond merely placing students with OCD in mainstream classrooms; it involves fostering genuine connections between these students and their peers. One effective strategy is the implementation of peer mentoring programs. These programs pair students with OCD with empathetic peers who can guide them through daily school life, offering support and friendship. This not only aids in reducing feelings of isolation among students with OCD but also promotes understanding and empathy among the general student population.

- Organizing inclusive group activities that encourage collaboration over competition, allowing students with OCD to participate fully without feeling overwhelmed or singled out.
- Training for teachers and staff on how to create a supportive classroom culture that values diversity and encourages all students to appreciate each other's unique contributions.
- Engagement with parents or caregivers to ensure strategies for social integration extend beyond the classroom and are reinforced at home.

Beyond structured programs, informal strategies such as encouraging participation in clubs or extracurricular activities aligned with the student's interests can provide natural opportunities for socialization. Schools can also host awareness events or workshops that educate the entire student body about OCD, demystifying the disorder and reducing stigma.

In conclusion, social integration strategies for students with OCD should be multifaceted, combining formal programs like peer mentoring with informal opportunities for engagement within the school community. By doing so, schools can create an environment where all students feel valued and supported, paving the way for meaningful friendships and social growth among those with OCD.

References:

- American Psychiatric Association. (2013). Diagnostic and Statistical Manual of Mental Disorders (5th ed.). Arlington, VA: American Psychiatric Publishing.

- U.S. Department of Education, Office of Special Education and Rehabilitative Services, Office of Special Education Programs. (2020). 40th Annual Report to Congress on the Implementation of the Individuals with Disabilities Education Act, 2018. Washington, D.C.

- Mancini, C., Van Ameringen, M., Oakman, J. M., & Figueiredo, C. (2016). Childhood attention deficit/hyperactivity disorder in adults with anxiety disorders. Psychological Medicine, 46(10), 2107-2115.

- Russell, A.J., Jassi, A., Fullana, M.A., Mack, H., Johnston, K., Heyman, I., Murphy, D.G.M., & Mataix-Cols D. (2013). Cognitive behavior therapy for comorbid obsessive-compulsive disorder in high-functioning autism spectrum disorders: A randomized controlled trial. Depression and Anxiety, 30(8), 697-708.

- School Mental Health Ontario. (n.d.). Supporting Students with Obsessive Compulsive Disorder: A Guide for School Personnel. Retrieved from https://smho-smso.ca/

10

Lifestyle Management

10.1 Diet, Exercise, and Sleep Hygiene

The interplay between diet, exercise, and sleep hygiene forms a cornerstone of effective lifestyle management, particularly for young boys grappling with Obsessive Compulsive Disorder (OCD). This triad not only influences physical health but also has profound implications on mental well-being. Understanding and optimizing these aspects can significantly contribute to managing OCD symptoms and enhancing overall quality of life.

Diet plays a pivotal role in mental health. Nutrient-rich foods support brain function and can mitigate some of the stress and anxiety associated with OCD. Incorporating a balanced diet that includes omega-3 fatty acids, antioxidants, vitamins, and minerals can aid in regulating mood and cognitive functions. Foods such as fatty fish, nuts, seeds, fruits, vegetables, and whole grains are beneficial. Conversely, reducing intake of processed foods, sugars, and caffeine is advisable as they can exacerbate anxiety levels.

Exercise is another critical component. Regular physical activity releases endorphins—natural mood lifters—that can alleviate symptoms of OCD by reducing stress and anxiety. Exercise also helps in improving sleep patterns which is crucial for individuals with OCD who often struggle with sleep disturbances. Activities like walking, cycling, swimming or team sports not only provide physical benefits but also offer opportunities for social interaction which is essential for emotional support.

Sleep hygiene refers to practices that promote regular, restful sleep patterns. Good sleep hygiene is vital for managing OCD as lack of sleep can worsen symptoms. Establishing a consistent bedtime routine that includes winding down activities without screen time an hour before bed can be helpful. Ensuring the sleeping environment is comfortable and free from distractions aids in improving sleep quality.

Additionally, limiting caffeine intake in the afternoon and evening contributes to better sleep patterns.
- Maintaining a balanced diet rich in nutrients supports brain health.
- Engaging in regular physical activity reduces stress and improves mood.
- Adopting good sleep hygiene practices enhances restorative sleep necessary for managing OCD effectively.

In conclusion, integrating healthy dietary habits with regular exercise routines and robust sleep hygiene practices creates a synergistic effect that bolsters both physical and mental health. For young boys facing the challenges of OCD, these lifestyle modifications can be empowering tools that complement therapeutic interventions like cognitive-behavioral therapy (CBT) or medication management strategies prescribed by healthcare professionals.

10.2 Managing Screen Time

In the context of lifestyle management for young boys with Obsessive Compulsive Disorder (OCD), managing screen time emerges as a crucial aspect, complementing diet, exercise, and sleep hygiene. The digital age has ushered in unparalleled access to information and connectivity but has also introduced challenges in maintaining mental well-being. Excessive screen time can exacerbate OCD symptoms by increasing anxiety, disrupting sleep patterns, and reducing opportunities for physical activity and face-to-face social interactions.

Screen time management is not about eliminating technology use entirely but finding a healthy balance that supports mental health while allowing young individuals to benefit from digital resources. It involves setting reasonable limits on the use of devices, prioritizing activities that promote physical health and real-world interactions over virtual engagement.

- Establishing clear guidelines for device usage can help in creating a structured environment where screen time is balanced with other activities.
- Encouraging hobbies that do not involve screens, such as sports, reading, or outdoor exploration, can provide healthy alternatives to digital entertainment.

- Promoting awareness about the impact of excessive screen use on mental health is essential for fostering self-regulation and responsible technology use.

Implementing "tech-free" zones or times at home can further support this balance. For instance, making bedrooms a screen-free area or setting aside specific times during the day for family activities without devices encourages better sleep hygiene and strengthens family bonds. Additionally, using apps or tools that track screen time can offer valuable insights into personal habits, enabling more informed decisions about digital consumption.

In conclusion, managing screen time is integral to lifestyle management for individuals with OCD. By establishing healthy boundaries around technology use, it's possible to mitigate some of the negative impacts associated with excessive screen exposure. This approach not only aids in reducing stress and anxiety but also enhances overall quality of life by promoting more meaningful engagements both offline and online.

10.3 Encouraging Hobbies and Interests

In the broader context of lifestyle management, particularly for young individuals navigating the complexities of Obsessive Compulsive Disorder (OCD), the encouragement of hobbies and interests stands out as a pivotal strategy. This approach not only diversifies their daily activities beyond the digital realm but also fosters a sense of accomplishment and personal growth. Engaging in hobbies can significantly dilute the intensity of OCD symptoms by channeling energy into productive and fulfilling endeavors.

The importance of nurturing hobbies and interests lies in their ability to provide an outlet for stress, enhance cognitive functions, and promote social interactions outside of screen-based activities. For instance, creative arts such as painting or writing offer a medium for self-expression and emotional release, while physical activities like sports or hiking contribute to improved physical health and mental clarity.

- Identifying personal interests that resonate with an individual's passions can lead to sustained engagement in these activities.

- Setting achievable goals within hobbies can enhance a sense of purpose and accomplishment, further motivating continued participation.
- Encouraging group activities or joining clubs can foster social connections, reducing feelings of isolation often associated with OCD.

Beyond merely suggesting alternatives to screen time, actively facilitating access to resources such as art supplies, musical instruments, or sports equipment can significantly lower barriers to entry for many hobbies. Additionally, celebrating milestones achieved within these pursuits reinforces positive behavior and cultivates an environment where personal interests are valued and pursued with vigor.

In conclusion, encouraging hobbies and interests forms a critical component of lifestyle management strategies aimed at mitigating OCD symptoms. By promoting balanced engagement in diverse activities, individuals are equipped with tools not just for distraction but for building resilience against compulsions. Ultimately, this leads to a richer quality of life characterized by enhanced well-being both mentally and physically.

References:

- American Psychiatric Association. (2013). Diagnostic and Statistical Manual of Mental Disorders (5th ed.). Arlington, VA: American Psychiatric Publishing. This manual provides comprehensive information on OCD and its management.

- Foa, E.B., Yadin, E., & Lichner, T.K. (2012). Exposure and Response (Ritual) Prevention for Obsessive-Compulsive Disorder: Therapist Guide (2nd ed.). Oxford University Press. This guide offers insights into one of the most effective treatments for OCD.

- Hyman, B.M., & Pedrick, C. (2005). The OCD Workbook: Your Guide to Breaking Free from Obsessive-Compulsive Disorder. New Harbinger Publications. A practical workbook providing strategies to cope with OCD.

- Saxena, S., & Maidment, K.M. (2004). Treatment of Compulsive Hoarding. Journal of Clinical Psychology, 60(11), 1143–1154. This article discusses the challenges and treatment strategies for compulsive hoarding, a condition often related to OCD.

11

Long-Term Management of OCD

1.1 Setting Realistic Expectations

The journey of managing Obsessive Compulsive Disorder (OCD) in young boys is a path filled with challenges and triumphs. A crucial step in this journey involves setting realistic expectations, not only for the children grappling with OCD but also for their parents, caregivers, and educators. Understanding what can be achieved over time with patience, persistence, and the right interventions is fundamental to fostering a supportive environment that encourages progress and resilience.

Realistic expectations begin with acknowledging that OCD is a chronic disorder; there's no quick fix or one-size-fits-all solution. Treatment and management are highly individualized processes that depend on the severity of the disorder, the specific symptoms experienced by the child, and how these symptoms impact their daily life. Recognizing this variability is key to setting achievable goals.

For parents and caregivers, it's essential to understand that progress may be slow and non-linear. There will be good days where it seems like significant strides are being made, followed by challenging days where old patterns resurface. This fluctuation is a normal part of recovery and doesn't signify failure or regression. Instead, it highlights the need for ongoing support, adaptation of strategies, and patience.

- Accepting that setbacks are part of the process helps in maintaining hope and perseverance.
- Emphasizing effort over perfection can encourage young boys to continue working on their coping strategies without fear of judgment or disappointment.
- Celebrating small victories along the way boosts morale and reinforces positive behavior changes.

In addition to managing expectations around treatment progress, it's also vital to have realistic views on social interactions and academic performance. OCD can significantly affect these areas of a child's life; thus, accommodations might be necessary. Parents should work closely with schools to ensure that these accommodations are provided in a way that supports the child's learning while minimizing stress.

Ultimately, setting realistic expectations involves embracing uncertainty and focusing on long-term well-being rather than immediate results. It means understanding that while OCD is part of their child's life, it doesn't define them or limit their potential for happiness and success. By adjusting expectations based on individual capabilities and celebrating every step forward, families can navigate OCD management more effectively, ensuring that young boys feel supported throughout their journey.

11.2 Preparing for Adolescence

The transition into adolescence marks a critical phase in the journey of managing Obsessive Compulsive Disorder (OCD) in young individuals. This period is characterized by significant physical, emotional, and social changes that can influence the course of OCD and its management. Preparing for adolescence involves understanding these changes and anticipating how they might impact a young person's OCD symptoms, as well as their overall well-being.

One of the key aspects of preparing for adolescence is recognizing the increased demand for independence that comes with this stage of life. Adolescents with OCD may face unique challenges as they strive for autonomy while navigating the complexities of their disorder. It's essential to foster an environment where they feel supported in taking on more responsibility for managing their symptoms, yet know that help is available when needed.

- Encouraging open communication about their experiences and feelings can help adolescents feel understood and less isolated.
- Providing education about OCD and its management during adolescence empowers young people to take an active role in their treatment.
- Adjusting treatment plans to accommodate the changing needs and preferences of adolescents ensures that interventions remain effective and relevant.

Social dynamics also undergo significant shifts during adolescence, which can affect individuals with

OCD in various ways. Peer relationships become increasingly important, and there may be heightened sensitivity to judgment or rejection related to OCD symptoms or behaviors. It's crucial to prepare adolescents by developing strategies to cope with potential social challenges, such as bullying or misunderstanding from peers.

- Teaching assertiveness skills can enable adolescents to advocate for themselves in social situations.
- Role-playing scenarios may help them practice how to explain their OCD to others in a way that fosters understanding rather than stigma.

Finally, academic pressures often intensify during adolescence, which can exacerbate stress and potentially trigger or worsen OCD symptoms. Collaborating with educational institutions to ensure appropriate accommodations are made is vital. This might include adjustments to workload, exam schedules, or classroom environments tailored to reduce stress without compromising educational goals.

In conclusion, preparing for adolescence with OCD requires a multifaceted approach that addresses the evolving psychological, social, and academic needs of young individuals. By proactively planning for these changes, parents, caregivers, and mental health professionals can support adolescents in navigating this challenging yet rewarding phase of life with resilience and confidence.

11.3 Transitioning to Adult Care

The transition from adolescence to adulthood is a pivotal period for individuals with Obsessive-Compulsive Disorder (OCD), marking a significant shift not only in personal and social responsibilities but also in the management of their healthcare. As young people with OCD move into adult care, they encounter a healthcare system that often operates under different principles than pediatric services. This transition requires careful planning, support, and adaptation strategies to ensure continuity of care and the maintenance of treatment gains achieved during childhood and adolescence.

One critical aspect of transitioning to adult care involves preparing the individual for changes in the patient-provider relationship. In pediatric settings, parents or guardians are heavily involved in decision-making processes; however, adult services emphasize patient autonomy and self-management. Young adults must adapt to taking on a more active role in their healthcare decisions, including advocating for their needs, scheduling appointments, and managing medication regimens.

- Developing self-advocacy skills is essential for navigating adult healthcare systems effectively.
- Transition programs that include skill-building workshops can empower young adults to take charge of their OCD management.
- Mental health professionals can facilitate this transition by introducing patients to adult-oriented resources and support networks.

Another challenge during this transition is ensuring continuity of care. Differences in treatment approaches between child/adolescent and adult mental health services can lead to gaps in care if not properly managed. It's crucial for current providers to collaborate with adult service providers well before the transition occurs, sharing comprehensive treatment histories and any insights into the individual's specific needs or preferences regarding therapy or medication.

- Creating a detailed transition plan that includes timelines, goals, and identified adult care providers can smooth the process.

- Maintaining open lines of communication between all parties involved—patient, family members, pediatric providers, and future adult providers—is key to a successful transition.

Facing the broader societal expectations associated with adulthood can exacerbate anxiety and OCD symptoms for some individuals. The combined stressors of managing OCD while navigating new roles as independent adults call for enhanced support systems that address both clinical needs and life skills development. Mental health professionals play a critical role in guiding young adults through these challenges by reinforcing coping strategies learned during adolescence and adapting them to new contexts encountered in adulthood.

- Peer support groups specifically tailored for young adults transitioning into adult care can provide valuable social support and shared learning opportunities.

- Ongoing psychoeducation about how various life transitions may impact OCD symptoms helps prepare individuals for potential challenges ahead.

In conclusion, transitioning to adult care is a complex process that requires strategic planning, collaboration among healthcare providers, skill development for young adults with OCD, and ongoing support tailored to their evolving needs. By addressing these elements comprehensively, stakeholders can facilitate smoother transitions into adult healthcare settings, promoting sustained well-being and effective management of OCD into adulthood.

References:

- Blount, R. L., & Anderson, D. (2018). The role of self-management in the transition from pediatric to adult health care: A review of the literature. Journal of Pediatric Psychology, 43(5), 459-475.
- Ginsburg, G. S., Becker, E. M., Keeton, C. P., Sakolsky, D., Piacentini, J., Albano, A. M., ... & Kendall, P. C. (2014). Naturalistic follow-up of youths

treated for pediatric anxiety disorders. JAMA Psychiatry, 71(3), 310-318.

- Piacentini, J., Bergman, R.L., Keller, M., & McCracken, J. (2003). Functional impairment in children and adolescents with obsessive-compulsive disorder. Journal of Child and Adolescent Psychopharmacology, 13(Suppl 1), S61-S69.

- Storch, E.A., Bussing, R., Small, B.J., Geffken, G.R., McNamara, J.P.H., Rahman, O., ... & Murphy, T.K. (2013). Randomized controlled trial of a cognitive-behavioral family intervention for pediatric obsessive-compulsive disorder. Journal of Consulting and Clinical Psychology, 81(6), 1101.

- Zohar, A.H. (2005). The epidemiology of obsessive-compulsive disorder in children and adolescents. Child and Adolescent Psychiatric Clinics of North America, 14(2), 187-203.

12

Stories of Hope and Recovery

12.1 Personal Success Stories

The inclusion of personal success stories in the narrative of overcoming Obsessive Compulsive Disorder (OCD) in young boys is not just a testament to resilience and courage; it serves as a beacon of hope for families navigating similar challenges. These stories underscore the importance of understanding, patience, and tailored interventions in fostering recovery and empowerment. By sharing real-life experiences, this section aims to illuminate the diverse pathways to managing OCD symptoms effectively, highlighting the pivotal role of support systems in facilitating positive outcomes.

One compelling narrative involves Alex, a 10-year-old boy who struggled with severe contamination fears that disrupted his daily life and education. Through a combination of Cognitive Behavioral Therapy (CBT) and Exposure Response Prevention (ERP), Alex gradually learned to confront his fears in a controlled environment. His journey underscores the significance of early intervention and the transformative power of therapy when coupled with family support. Alex's story is not just about overcoming OCD; it's about reclaiming childhood.

Another inspiring account features Ben, whose obsessive thoughts led to ritualistic behaviors that consumed hours of his day. Feeling isolated from his peers, Ben's turning point came when he began to engage in group therapy sessions designed for young individuals with OCD. Here, Ben found solace in shared experiences and learned coping strategies that resonated with him personally. This communal aspect of recovery highlights how peer support can complement traditional therapies by providing social connections and reducing stigma.

- Early diagnosis and intervention are crucial for effective management.
- Therapeutic approaches like CBT and ERP can be transformative.

- Support from families, therapists, and peers plays an indispensable role in recovery.

In conclusion, these personal success stories serve as powerful examples of how young boys with OCD can not only navigate their condition but also thrive despite it. They emphasize the importance of personalized care plans that include both professional therapies and supportive community networks. By sharing these narratives, "OCD in Young Boys: Obsessive Compulsive Disorder In Boys Survival Guide" aims to foster a deeper understanding of OCD while offering hope and practical strategies for families facing similar struggles.

12.2 Lessons Learned from Families

The journey of families navigating the complexities of Obsessive Compulsive Disorder (OCD) in young boys offers invaluable insights into the resilience and adaptability required to support recovery. The experiences of these families underscore a multifaceted approach to managing OCD, emphasizing not just clinical interventions but also the nurturing role of the family environment. This section delves into the lessons learned from families who have walked this path, shedding light on strategies that foster hope and facilitate healing.

One critical lesson is the importance of creating an open and supportive home atmosphere where feelings and fears can be discussed without judgment. Families that encourage open communication tend to navigate the challenges of OCD with greater success. This openness helps in demystifying the disorder, making it less daunting for both the child and their family members. It also positions family members as allies in the child's recovery journey, rather than bystanders or enforcers of therapy protocols.

Another key insight is the significance of educating oneself about OCD. Knowledge empowers families to understand the nuances of OCD symptoms and treatments, enabling them to make informed decisions about care and interventions. It also prepares them to advocate effectively for their child in educational settings, ensuring that necessary accommodations are made to support their learning and social integration.

- Embracing flexibility in daily routines to accommodate therapy sessions or coping mechanisms without adding stress.

- Leveraging community resources such as support groups for parents and siblings, which provide a shared space for learning and emotional support.
- Recognizing and celebrating small victories along the recovery path, reinforcing positive behaviors and progress.

In conclusion, families play a pivotal role in shaping the recovery trajectory for young boys with OCD. The lessons learned from these courageous families highlight a holistic approach that blends professional treatment with a compassionate, informed family environment. By sharing these insights, we aim not only to offer practical strategies but also to inspire hope among families facing similar challenges.

12.3 Building a Future Full of Possibility

The journey from understanding and managing Obsessive Compulsive Disorder (OCD) within the family context to envisioning a future full of possibility represents a significant transition. This phase is not just about coping with the present but also about laying the groundwork for a life that transcends the limitations often imposed by OCD. It's about fostering an environment where young individuals feel empowered to dream big, pursue their passions, and achieve their full potential despite the challenges they face.

Building such a future requires a concerted effort from both families and professionals to instill hope and resilience in these young minds. It involves creating opportunities for them to explore their interests and talents, which can sometimes be overshadowed by the demands of therapy and management of OCD symptoms. Encouraging participation in activities outside of the therapeutic context can provide a sense of normalcy and achievement, crucial for building self-esteem and social skills.

- Integrating technology as a tool for independence, using apps designed to manage time or tasks can foster a sense of control over one's life.
- Developing personalized strategies that align with individual strengths, thereby making daily challenges more manageable and less intimidating.

- Promoting educational paths that accommodate learning differences, ensuring that academic pursuits are not hindered by OCD.

This approach also emphasizes the importance of community involvement. Engaging with support networks outside the immediate family can offer new perspectives and resources that enrich the recovery process. These networks can include peer groups, online forums, or local organizations dedicated to mental health awareness. Such connections not only broaden social circles but also normalize experiences, reducing feelings of isolation or difference among affected individuals.

In conclusion, building a future full of possibility for young boys with OCD is an achievable goal when approached with creativity, patience, and persistence. By focusing on strengths rather than limitations, families together with healthcare providers can pave the way for fulfilling lives marked by personal achievements and happiness beyond OCD.

References:

- American Psychiatric Association. (2013). Diagnostic and Statistical Manual of Mental Disorders (5th ed.). Arlington, VA: American Psychiatric Publishing.

- March, J.S., & Benton, C.M. (2007). Treating Obsessive-Compulsive Disorder in Children and Adolescents: A Cognitive-Behavioral Approach. New York: Guilford Press.

- Foa, E.B., Yadin, E., & Lichner, T.K. (2012). Exposure and Response (Ritual) Prevention for Obsessive Compulsive Disorder: Therapist Guide (2nd ed.). Oxford University Press.

- Menzies, R.G., & de Silva, P. (2003). Obsessive-Compulsive Disorder: Theory, Research and Treatment. Wiley.

- National Institute of Mental Health. (2020). Obsessive-Compulsive Disorder. Retrieved from https://www.nimh.nih.gov/health/topics/obsessive-compulsive-disorder-ocd

"OCD in Young Boys: Obsessive Compulsive Disorder In Boys Survival Guide" is a pivotal non-fiction work aimed at providing crucial support for parents, caregivers, and educators dealing with Obsessive Compulsive Disorder (OCD) in young boys. This guide delves into the unique challenges that boys with OCD face, offering practical advice, strategies, and insights to aid their development and well-being. The book starts by demystifying OCD—detailing its symptoms, causes, and specific manifestations in boys—using a mix of scientific research and personal narratives to illustrate its impact on their lives.

Central to the guide is the emphasis on creating a supportive environment that nurtures resilience and positive coping mechanisms. It offers detailed strategies for fostering such an environment at home and underscores the importance of collaborative efforts between families and professionals in seeking treatment and accommodations in educational settings. A significant focus is placed on empowerment, equipping readers with tools to help young boys understand their condition, communicate their experiences, and engage actively in their treatment plans. Techniques like cognitive-behavioral therapy (CBT), exposure-response prevention (ERP), mindfulness, and relaxation exercises are explained in accessible terms.

The book also confronts common misconceptions about OCD and societal stigmas, advocating for open discussions about mental health to create a more understanding society. Additionally, it outlines community resources like support groups, online forums, and workshops that can offer further support. "OCD in Young Boys" emerges as an invaluable resource for those committed to aiding young boys through their OCD journey with empathy, evidence-based strategies, hope, and healing.

Made in United States
North Haven, CT
03 May 2025